Houghton
Mifflin
Harcourt

NATIONAL JOURNEYS

Program Consultants

Shervaughnna Anderson · Marty Hougen

Carol Jago · Erik Palmer · Shane Templeton

Sheila Valencia · MaryEllen Vogt

Consulting Author · Irene Fountas

Unit 5

Watch Us Grow 9

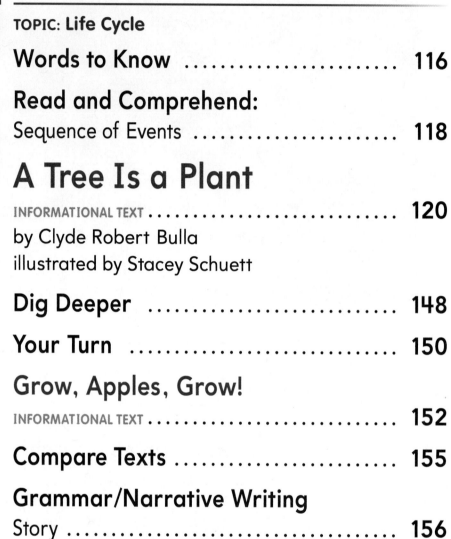

Lesson
25

TOPIC: **Learning About Our Country**

Be a Reading Detective!

Welcome, Reader!

Your help is needed to find clues in texts. As a **Reading Detective**, you will need to **ask lots of questions.** You will also need to **read carefully.**

myNotebook

As you read, mark up the text. Save your work to **myNotebook**.

- Highlight details.
- Add notes and questions.
- Add new words to **myWordList**.

- Use letters and sounds you know to help you read the words.
- Look at the pictures.
- Think about what is happening.

Let's go!

UNIT 5

Watch Us Grow

Stream to Start

> 66 As things grow, they also change. 99
>
> — Anonymous

Performance Task Preview

At the end of this unit, you will write a story. The characters will be animals from two of the texts you read! In your story, you will use details from the texts.

hmhfyi.com

Channel One News®

9

🔍 LANGUAGE DETECTIVE

Talk About Words
Work with a partner.
Take turns asking and
answering questions
about the photos. Use
the blue words in your
questions and answers.

myNotebook

Add new words to
myWordList. Use them
in your speaking
and writing.

Words to Know

Read Together

▶ Read each Context Card.

▶ Choose two blue words.
Use them in sentences.

1 **few**
There are only a few
trees here.

2 **night**
The buds open in the
day and close at night.

3 loudly

The bird sang loudly in the tree.

4 window

The big tree is very close to the window.

5 noise

I heard a noise in the garden.

6 story

He tells a story about planting trees.

7 shall

We shall pick apples today.

8 world

My garden is the best place in the world.

Read and Comprehend

☑ **TARGET SKILL**

Story Structure The parts of a story work together. **Characters** are the people and animals. The **setting** is when and where a story takes place. Events make up the **plot.** The plot is often about a problem and how characters solve it. A story map can help you tell about the different parts.

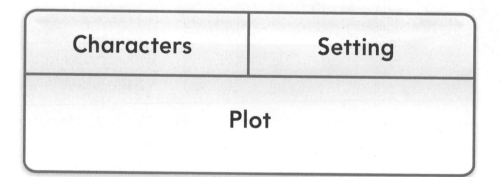

Characters	Setting
Plot	

☑ **TARGET STRATEGY**

Analyze/Evaluate Tell how you think and feel about the story. Use text evidence to tell why.

Gardens

To make a garden grow, start with seeds. Plant them in the soil. Then, make sure they have enough water and sunlight. Soon, the seeds will start to grow. Tiny plants will pop up. After that, you will have big plants with flowers or vegetables.

You will read a story about a character named Toad who plants seeds in **The Garden.**

Talk About It

What do you know about growing plants? What would you like to know? Share your ideas. Listen carefully. What did you learn from others?

13

ANCHOR TEXT

✓ GENRE

A **fantasy** is a story that could not happen in real life. Look for:

▸ animals who talk and act like people
▸ events that could not really happen

Meet the Author and Illustrator

Arnold Lobel

Arnold Lobel started drawing when he was a child. When he grew up, he wrote and illustrated almost 100 books for children. His books won many awards. Frog and Toad have even been in a Broadway musical!

The Garden
from Frog and Toad Together
by Arnold Lobel

ESSENTIAL QUESTION

What grows in
a garden?

Frog was in his garden.

Toad came walking by.

"What a fine garden you have, Frog,"
he said.

"Yes," said Frog.   "It is very nice,
but it was hard work."

"I wish I had a garden," said Toad.

"Here are some flower seeds.

Plant them in the ground," said Frog,

"and soon you will have a garden."

"How soon?" asked Toad.

"Quite soon," said Frog.

Toad ran home.

He planted the flower seeds.

"Now seeds," said Toad, "start growing."

Toad walked up and down a few times.

The seeds did not start to grow.

Toad put his head
close to the ground
and said loudly,
"Now seeds, start growing!"
Toad looked at the ground again.
The seeds did not start to grow.

Toad put his head
very close to the ground
and shouted,
"NOW SEEDS, START GROWING!"
Frog came running up the path.
"What is all this noise?" he asked.
"My seeds will not grow," said Toad.
"You are shouting too much," said Frog.
"These poor seeds are afraid to grow."
"My seeds are afraid to grow?" asked Toad.

ANALYZE THE TEXT

Repetition What words are
repeated on these pages? Why?

"Of course," said Frog.

"Leave them alone for a few days.

Let the sun shine on them,

let the rain fall on them.

Soon your seeds will start to grow."

That night
Toad looked out of his window.
"Drat!" said Toad.
"My seeds have not
started to grow.
They must be afraid of the dark."
Toad went out to his garden
with some candles.
"I will read the seeds a story,"
said Toad.
"Then they will not be afraid."
Toad read a long story to his seeds.

ANALYZE THE TEXT

Story Structure What is Toad's problem? How is he trying to solve it?

All the next day
Toad sang songs
to his seeds.

And all the next day
Toad read poems
to his seeds.

And all the next day
Toad played music
for his seeds.

Toad looked at the ground.
The seeds still did not
start to grow.
"What shall I do?" cried Toad.
"These must be
the most frightened seeds
in the whole world!"

Then Toad felt very tired,
and he fell asleep.

"Toad, Toad, wake up," said Frog.
"Look at your garden!"
Toad looked at his garden.
Little green plants were coming up
out of the ground.

"At last," shouted Toad,
"my seeds have stopped
being afraid to grow!"
"And now you will have
a nice garden too," said Frog.

"Yes," said Toad,
"but you were right, Frog.
It was very hard work."

Dig Deeper

Read Together

Use Clues to Analyze the Text

Use these pages to learn about Story Structure and Repetition. Then read **The Garden** again.

Story Structure

Frog and Toad are the **characters** in **The Garden**. What kind of place is the **setting** of this story? Does the story happen during the day, at night, or both? Think about the problem Toad has and how it is solved. Use a story map to write text evidence about the characters, setting, and important events.

Characters	Setting
Plot

Repetition

Authors sometimes use the same words or same kind of event over and over in a story. This is called **repetition.** This can make the story fun to read. It can also help you understand what is important in the story.

Look at page 24. What does Toad do over and over? Why do you think the author uses the words **all the next day** more than once?

Your Turn

RETURN TO THE ESSENTIAL QUESTION

Turn and Talk

What grows in a garden? Talk with a small group. Then talk about the problem Toad has when he tries to grow his garden. How is it solved? Use details from text evidence to explain your ideas and feelings clearly.

Classroom Conversation

Talk about these questions with your class.

1. Describe what Toad does to get his seeds to grow. What really makes them grow?

2. How does Frog help Toad?

3. What would you plant in a garden? How would you take care of the garden?

WRITE ABOUT READING ....

Response Write a book report about **The Garden**. Begin by telling the name of the story and what it is mainly about. Then tell what you like about it. Give reasons why. Tell what you don't like. Give reasons why.

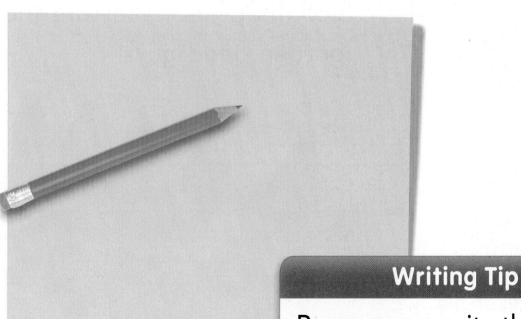

Writing Tip

Be sure you write the word **I** with a capital letter.

Garden Good Guys
by Timothy Thomas

☑ **GENRE**

Informational text gives facts about a topic. Find facts about insects that help gardens in this selection.

☑ **TEXT FOCUS**

Labels are words that tell more about the pictures in a text. They can name parts of the picture or the whole picture. Look for labels. What information do they give?

If you have a garden, you should know about bugs. Some bugs are pests that eat the plants. Other bugs eat the pests. They are the garden good guys!

If you want a healthy garden, make sure you have **ladybugs**. Ladybugs eat tiny bugs that snack on garden plants.

You may not think a **praying mantis** is as pretty as a ladybug, but it is a good garden friend. A praying mantis hunts and eats many garden pests.

ladybug

praying mantis

big-eyed bug

The **big-eyed bug** is tiny. Can you guess how it got its name? Big-eyed bugs eat bugs that harm vegetables.

The **dragonfly** has a long thin body, large eyes, and two sets of wings. Dragonflies are good for gardens and good for you, too. They eat garden pests <u>and</u> mosquitoes!

wing

dragonfly

Compare Texts

Read Together

TEXT TO TEXT

Compare Gardens Think about the gardens in both selections. What helps each garden grow?

TEXT TO SELF

Connect to Experiences Think about how Toad cared for his garden. Write about something you have cared for.

TEXT TO WORLD

Think and Share Tell a partner why people should help plants grow. Take turns speaking. Listen to each other.

Grammar

Subject Pronouns Words that can take the place of nouns are called **pronouns**. The pronouns **he**, **she**, and **it** name one. The pronouns **we** and **they** name more than one.

Read
Together

Ben watered the tree.
He watered the tree.

The tree grew.
It grew.

Birds loved the tree.
They loved the tree.

Lily fed the birds.
She fed the birds.

Choose the correct pronoun to name each picture.
Write it on a sheet of paper. Then say a sentence
to a partner about each picture. Use the pronoun.

1. she   he

2. they   it

3. it   we

4. they   she

5. we   he

Connect Grammar to Writing

When you proofread your writing, be sure
you have used pronouns correctly.

Narrative Writing

✔ **Development** **Dialogue** shows the exact words characters say. Niki wrote about what Frog and Toad did next in the story. Then she added words that told what they said.

Revised Draft

"May I pick some flowers?"

asked Frog. Toad said, "Yes!"
∧ Frog and Toad both wanted

to pick flowers.

Writing Checklist

✔ **Development** Did I write the exact words characters say?

✔ Did I use time-order words to tell when events happen?

✔ Did I use pronouns correctly?

Look for story events and the exact words Frog and Toad say in Niki's final copy. Then revise your own writing. Use the Checklist.

Final Copy

Picking Flowers

Frog really liked Toad's new garden. "May I pick some flowers?" asked Frog. Toad said, "Yes!" Frog and Toad both wanted to pick flowers. First, they found a nice flower vase. Then they went outside and picked all kinds of flowers. "Frog, you are a good friend. Thank you for helping me grow my flowers," said Toad.

Lesson 22

LANGUAGE DETECTIVE

Talk About Words
Work with a partner. Use the blue words in complete sentences to tell about something you did.

Words to Know

Read Together

▶ Read each **Context Card**.

▶ Make up a new sentence that uses a blue word.

1 learning
This baby giraffe is learning how to walk.

2 begins
The lion cub begins to get stronger.

42

3 until

These owls can't fly until they are older.

4 eight

The eight little swans go for a swim.

5 young

The young hippo will be very big soon.

6 follow

The bear cubs follow their mother.

7 years

An elephant can live for seventy years.

8 baby

This baby panda is eating plants.

Read and Comprehend

☑ **TARGET SKILL**

Conclusions Sometimes authors do not tell all the details. Readers must use text evidence from the words and pictures and think about what they already know to make a smart guess about what the author does not tell. This smart guess is a **conclusion.** Use a chart to write details and conclusions about what you read.

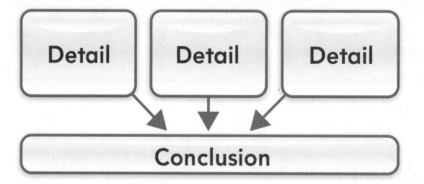

☑ **TARGET STRATEGY**

Visualize As you read, picture in your mind what is happening to help you understand.

Animals

Animals have special body parts that help them do amazing things. Kangaroos have strong legs that help them jump very far. Some monkeys can use their tails to hang from branches. Anteaters have long noses they use to grab insects under the dirt. You will read more interesting facts about animals in **Amazing Animals.**

Think | Write | Pair | Share

Think about an amazing animal. Why is it amazing? Complete the sentence:

___ is amazing because ___.

Share with a partner. Act out what makes the animal amazing.

ANCHOR TEXT

Amazing Animals

Informational text gives facts. As you read, look for:
- ▸ information and facts in the words
- ▸ photos that show real animals

Meet the Author

Gwendolyn Hooks

Gwendolyn Hooks wrote this story because she loves animals. "This story is about wild animals," she explains.
"I don't own any wild animals, but I do have a pet cat."

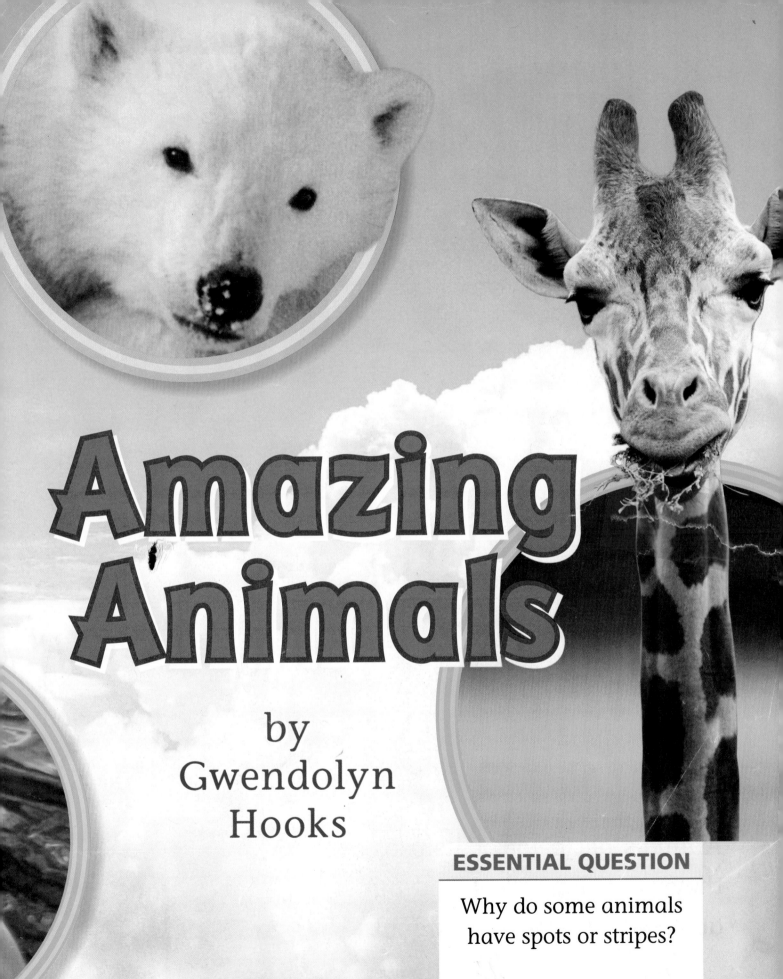

Amazing Animals

by
Gwendolyn
Hooks

ESSENTIAL QUESTION

Why do some animals
have spots or stripes?

Big eyes,

long beak,

thick fur,

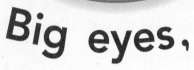

big squeak!

Animals get a lot of help as they grow up. Let's find out about eight amazing animals.

Polar Bear

A polar bear has thick fur. Each hair is like a tube. The hair has no color, like glass. The sun makes it look white.

How does thick, white fur help?

ANALYZE THE TEXT

Conclusions How do you think the color of their fur helps polar bears?

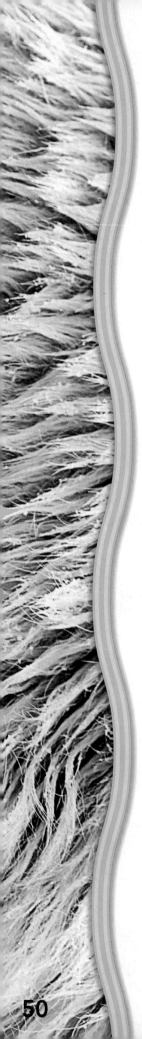

Thick fur helps polar bears stay warm. The color of their fur looks the same as snow. This helps them hide.

Where does this cute young polar bear like to hide?

Elephant

An elephant has a long nose. The nose is called a trunk. It takes many years for an elephant to grow two big teeth. These teeth are called tusks.

How do tusks and a trunk help?

51

ANALYZE THE TEXT

Using Context What are **tusks**? How do elephants use their tusks?

Elephants use their tusks to scrape bark off trees. Then they eat the bark. These elephants are learning to use their trunks to get water.

Sometimes they will spray water at a friend!

Camel

Some camels have one hump.
Some have two. All camels
have two rows of eyelashes.

How do humps and thick
eyelashes help?

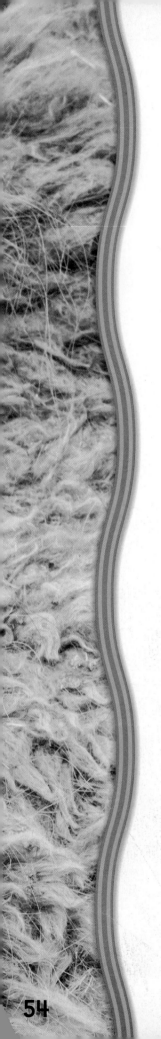

A camel's hump has fat inside. On long trips, a camel's body uses the fat for food. A camel's eyelashes keep out the desert sand.

This **baby** camel will **follow** his mother when the herd goes from place to place.

Duck

A duck is a bird. It has two feet, and each foot has three toes. A duck has a beak, too.

How do feet and a beak help?

Ducks use their feet to swim in the water or walk on land. They use their beaks to eat plants and bugs.

Look! This duck uses her beak to clean her friend.

Giraffe

A giraffe has spots. A giraffe has a long neck.

How do spots and a long neck help?

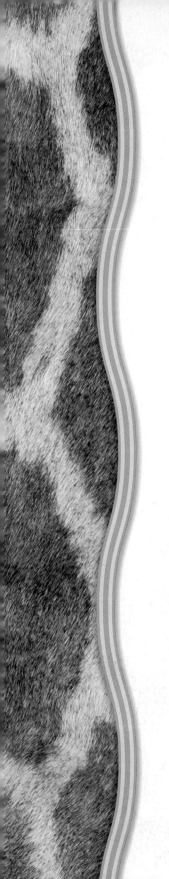

A giraffe's spots help it hide. A
giraffe's long neck helps it reach
the leaves of trees.

This giraffe's long neck helps her
reach her baby. She gives him a
big kiss!

Porcupine

A porcupine has soft quills when it is born. The quills get sharp in a day or two.

How do quills help?

Quills help keep a porcupine safe. If an animal begins to come too close, the porcupine backs into it. The sharp quills hurt!

Quills tell this cub to stay away!

Turtle

A turtle has a shell that is very hard.

How does a hard shell help?

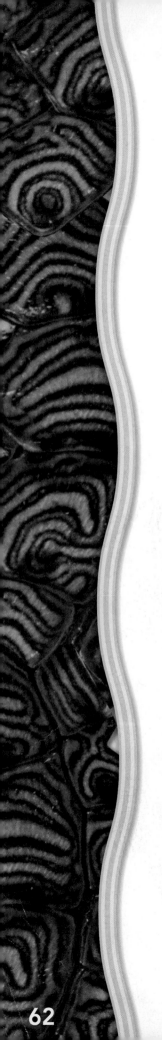

A turtle can hide inside its shell from an animal that may hurt it. The turtle waits until the animal goes away. Then the turtle comes back out.

You're safe now, turtle!

Dolphin

A dolphin's tail has two parts called flukes. A dolphin has two flippers.

How do tail flukes and flippers help?

A dolphin flips its tail flukes up
and down to swim fast. It uses its
flippers to turn to the left or right.

These two dolphins swim away fast.
Who will be first?

Have fun, dolphins!

Dig Deeper

Use Clues to Analyze the Text

Use these pages to learn about Conclusions and Using Context. Then read **Amazing Animals** again.

Conclusions

Use text evidence from **Amazing Animals** to draw **conclusions** about what the author does not say. The author does not tell you what it is like where polar bears live. What do the pictures show? Which words help you? What else do you know about polar bears? Use a chart to write your conclusions.

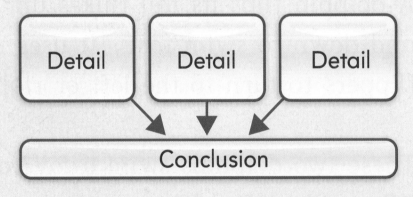

Using Context

An author may use words you do not know. Read the other words in the sentence and look at the picture to help you figure out the word.

What does **trunk** mean in the selection? The words **long nose** and the picture of the elephants are clues that tell you the **trunk** is the long part of an elephant's face. Another good clue is the sentence **The nose is called a trunk.**

Your Turn

RETURN TO THE ESSENTIAL QUESTION

Turn and Talk

Why do some animals have spots or stripes?
Talk about how and why some animals in **Amazing Animals** hide. Use text evidence to explain your ideas clearly. Ask questions to understand your partner's ideas.

 Classroom Conversation

Talk about these questions with your class.

1 How do some animals stay safe?

2 How does a dolphin's tail help it live?

3 Tell about some parts other animals have that help them. How do your hands help you?

Performance Task

Response Which is the most amazing animal in **Amazing Animals?** Draw a picture of it and label its body parts. Use text evidence to write reasons why the animal is amazing. Tell how special body parts help that animal.

Writing Tip

Use words like **because** or **so** to show how your opinion and reasons go together.

FOLKTALE

Read Together

The Ugly Duckling

Once upon a time, a duck sat on eight eggs. One day, all but one of the eggs hatched. The ducks waited until the last baby bird came out. He was big and gray. The other ducks thought he was ugly.

Each day the ducklings would follow Mother Duck. They were learning to be ducks. The other ducks did not want to play with the ugly duckling. He felt sad. One day he left.

Winter soon came. A farmer found the ugly duckling. "I must take you home before it begins to snow," he said.

When spring came, the farmer took the duckling to a pond. The duckling saw himself in the water. He felt like many years had passed. He had changed!

Now he knew he was not an ugly duckling. He was a young swan. He and the other swans lived happily ever after.

Compare Texts

Read Together

TEXT TO TEXT

Compare Selections Which selection is true? Which is make-believe? Tell a small group how you know. Use text evidence to help you explain.

TEXT TO SELF

Think About Characters How does the duckling in **The Ugly Duckling** change in the story? Tell how you have changed since you were a baby.

TEXT TO WORLD

Connect to Science Pick an animal. How does it grow? Use books and other sources to find out.

Grammar

The Pronouns **I** and **Me** Use **I** in the subject of a sentence and **me** in the predicate. Name yourself last when you talk about yourself and others.

Read Together

Correct

Sara and I like baby animals.

Not Correct

I and Sara like baby animals.
Me and Sara like baby animals.

Correct

The puppy licks **Jill and me.**

Not Correct

The puppy licks **me and Jill.**
The puppy licks **Jill and I.**

74

Write the correct words to finish each
sentence. Use another sheet of paper.
Read your sentences to a partner.

1. _____**?**_____ saw a piglet.
 Dad and I   I and Dad

2. The chicks looked at _____**?**_____.
 Jake and me   me and Jake

3. _____**?**_____ fed one kitten.
 I and Ana   Ana and I

4. The cubs ran from _____**?**_____.
 Liz and I   Liz and me

Connect Grammar to Writing

When you proofread your writing, be sure
to use the pronouns **I** and **me** correctly.
Remember to capitalize **I.**

Narrative Writing

☑ **Development** Good **story sentences** have exact verbs that help readers picture what the story characters are doing.

Troy wrote about a baby bird. Later, he changed **went** to a more exact verb.

Revised Draft

Then Jay ~~went~~ into the air.
            flew
            ^

Writing Checklist

☑ **Development** Do my sentences have exact verbs?

☑ Did I tell what happened in order?

☑ Do I need to delete any words?

☑ Does my last sentence tell the ending?

Final Copy

Flying Lesson

Jay stood quietly by the nest.

First, he watched his mom.

Then Jay flew into the air.

He sailed high above the garden.

Jay soared all the way home.

77

LANGUAGE DETECTIVE

Talk About Words
Nouns are words that name people, animals, things, or places. Work with a partner. Find the blue words that are nouns. Use them in complete sentences. Add details to your sentences to tell more about the nouns.

Words to Know

Read Together

▶ Read each **Context Card**.

▶ Ask a question that uses one of the blue words.

1 **house**
They learned how to build a house for birds.

2 **along**
He rode carefully along the bike path.

3 together

The baby can clap her hands together now.

4 boy

The boy teaches his sister to read.

5 father

My father teaches me how to swim.

6 again

We went out on the ice again to practice.

7 nothing

At first nothing fit, but he finished the puzzle.

8 began

She began to take violin lessons.

Read and Comprehend

☑ **TARGET SKILL**

Cause and Effect Sometimes one story event causes another event to happen. The **cause** happens first. The **effect** is what happens next. As you read, ask yourself what happens and why. You can use a chart to help you understand events.

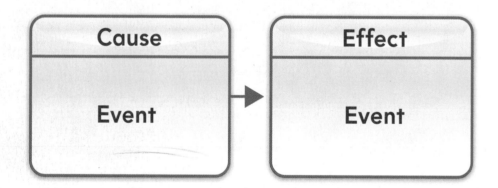

Cause	Effect
Event	Event

☑ **TARGET STRATEGY**

Monitor/Clarify If a part doesn't make sense, you can ask questions, reread, and use the pictures for help.

Pets

A pet can be a good friend. A cat can cuddle. A dog can play with a ball. What kinds of pets do you know about? Have you ever had a pet? Pets need care. They need to be fed. Some need to be walked. You will read about a boy and his pet dog in **Whistle for Willie.**

Think | Pair | Share

What pet would you like best? Think about it. Finish the sentences. Share with a partner:

I would like ___ .

I would not like ___.

___ is better than ___.

ANCHOR TEXT

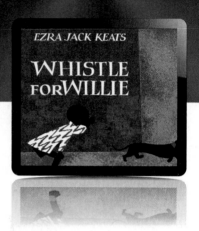

EZRA JACK KEATS

WHISTLE FOR WILLIE

✓ GENRE

Realistic fiction is a story that could happen in real life. As you read, look for:

▸ events that could really happen

▸ characters who do things real people and animals do

Meet the Author and Illustrator

Ezra Jack Keats

Ezra Jack Keats wrote and illustrated books for children. When Mr. Keats was a boy, he drew pictures on the kitchen table. His mother was so proud, she kept the art rather than wash the table.

WHISTLE FOR WILLIE

by Ezra Jack Keats

Oh, how Peter wished he could whistle!

He saw a boy playing with his dog. Whenever the boy whistled, the dog ran straight to him.

ANALYZE THE TEXT

Cause and Effect What happens when the boy whistles?

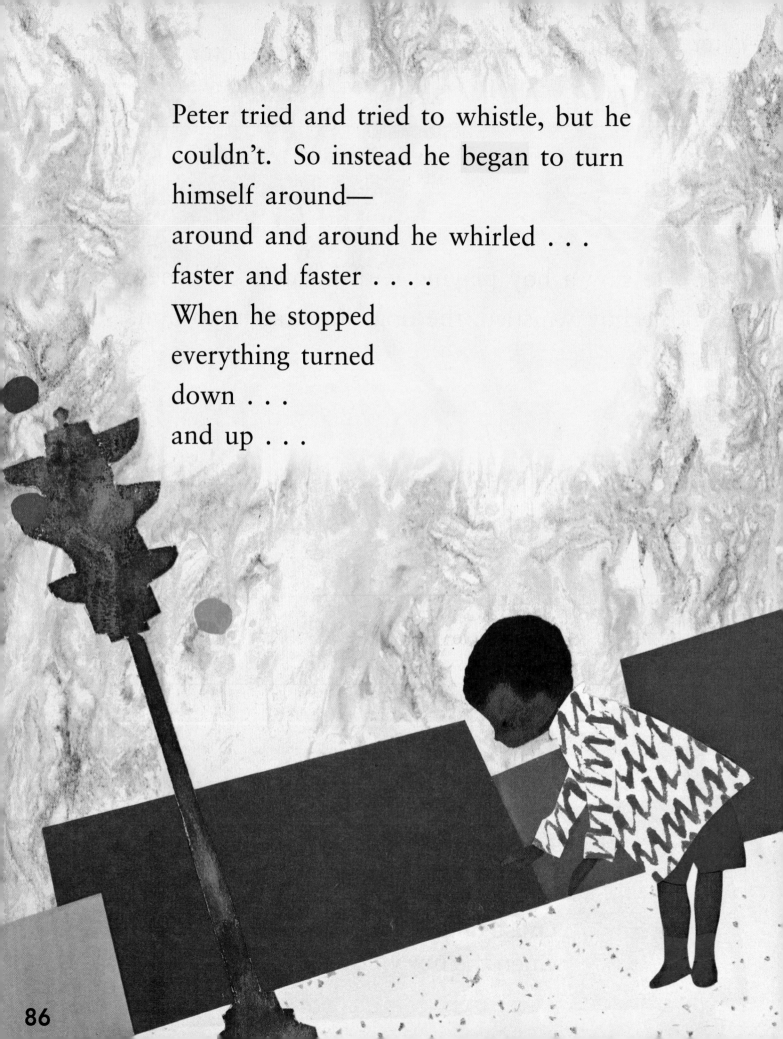

Peter tried and tried to whistle, but he
couldn't. So instead he began to turn
himself around—
around and around he whirled . . .
faster and faster . . . .
When he stopped
everything turned
down . . .
and up . . .

and up . . .
and down . . .
and around
and around.

Peter saw his dog, Willie, coming. Quick as a wink, he hid in an empty carton lying on the sidewalk.

ANALYZE THE TEXT

Figurative Language What does **quick as a wink** mean? Why do you think so?

"Wouldn't it be funny if I whistled?" Peter thought. "Willie would stop and look all around to see who it was."

Peter tried again to whistle—but still he couldn't. So Willie just walked on.

Peter got out of the carton and started home.
On the way he took some colored chalks out
of his pocket and drew a long, long line
right up to his door.

He stood there and tried to whistle
again. He blew till his cheeks were
tired. But nothing happened.

He went into his house and put on his father's old hat to make himself feel more grown-up. He looked into the mirror to practice whistling. Still no whistle!

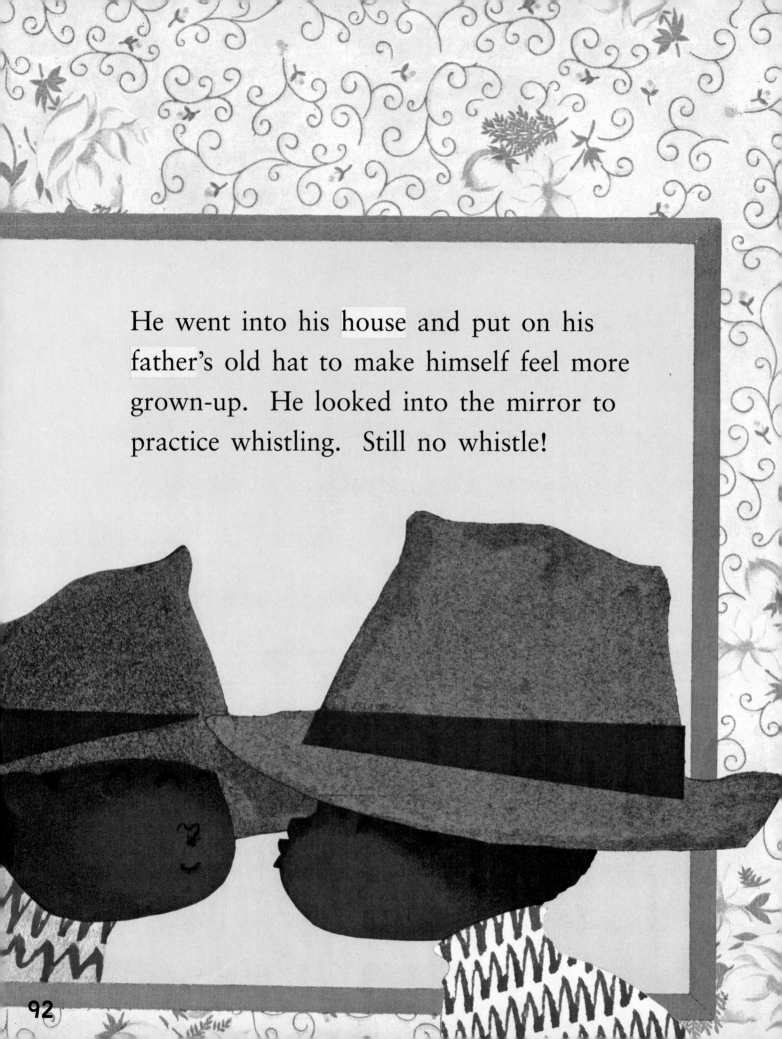

When his mother saw what he was doing,
Peter pretended that he was his father.
He said, "I've come home early today, dear.
Is Peter here?"
His mother answered, "Why no, he's outside
with Willie."
"Well, I'll go out and look for them," said Peter.

First he walked along a crack in the
sidewalk. Then he tried to run away
from his shadow.

He jumped off his shadow.
But when he landed
they were
together
again.

He came to the corner
where the carton was,
and who should he see
but Willie!

Peter scrambled under the carton.
He blew and blew.
Suddenly—out came a real whistle!

Willie stopped and looked around to
see who it was.

"It's me," Peter shouted, and stood up.
Willie raced straight to him.

Peter ran home to show his father and
mother what he could do.
They loved Peter's whistling. So did Willie.

Peter's mother asked him and Willie
to go on an errand to the grocery store.
He whistled all the way there,
and he whistled all the way home.

Dig Deeper

Use Clues to Analyze the Text

Use these pages to learn about Cause and Effect and Figurative Language. Then read **Whistle for Willie** again.

Cause and Effect

In **Whistle for Willie**, story events cause other events to happen. The **cause** is the reason why something else happens. The **effect** is what happens next. In the story, Peter keeps trying to whistle. This is the cause. What happens because he tries to whistle? Use a chart like this to show why important events happen.

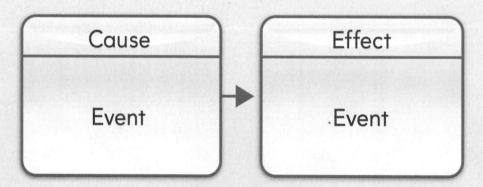

Cause		Effect
Event	→	Event

Figurative Language

Authors often use words in interesting ways to help you picture what is happening. The story says that Peter **scrambled under** the carton when he sees Willie. These words help you know how Peter moves. He does not go under the carton slowly. He goes under very quickly. What other words does the author use in interesting ways?

Your Turn

RETURN TO THE ESSENTIAL QUESTION

 Turn and Talk

How can you take good care of a pet? How does Peter take care of Willie? Use text evidence to help you explain. Talk about what you know about taking care of a pet. Tell your ideas clearly.

Classroom Conversation

Talk about these questions with your class.

1 What lesson can you learn from Peter?

2 Why does Peter want to learn to whistle?

3 Peter learns how to whistle. What have you learned how to do because you kept trying?

WRITE ABOUT READING ·················

Response What would Willie say if he could talk? What would he say happened? Write sentences that tell the story the way Willie would tell it.

Writing Tip

Use words like **first, next, then,** and **finally** to tell when things happen.

Read Together

✅ GENRE

Poetry uses words to describe pictures and feelings. Listen for interesting words in each poem. Clap along with the rhythm, or beat.

✅ TEXT FOCUS

Words **rhyme** if they have the same ending sound. Which poems use words that rhyme?

Pet Poems

This poem began as a folk song. Read it along with your class. Then sing it together.

Bingo

There was a farmer had a dog,
And Bingo was his name, O!
B – I – N – G – O,
B – I – N – G – O,
B – I – N – G – O,

And Bingo was his name, O!

Can someone in your class read this poem in Spanish? Now read it again in English.

Caballito blanco, reblanco

Caballito blanco,
reblanco,
sácame de aquí,
llévame hasta el puerto
donde yo nací.

Little White Horse

Little horse
White as snow
Take me where
I long to go.
Take me to the port
By the sea
Where I was born
And long to be.

traditional folk poem

What kind of pet would you like to have? Would you like a furry pet or a pet with scales?

PET SNAKE

No trace of fuzz.
No bit of fur.
No growling bark,
or gentle purr.
No cozy cuddle.
No sloppy kiss.
All he really does
is hisssssssssss.

by Rebecca Kai Dotlich

Respond to Poetry

Write a pet poem. Use words with the same beginning sounds and rhyming words. Memorize a poem or song. Use your voice to show how it makes you feel.

Compare Texts

Read Together

TEXT TO TEXT

Compare Pets How is Willie different from the pet snake in the poem? Write words that tell what Willie looks like and what he can do. Draw a picture.

TEXT TO SELF

Describe a Pet Find words in the poems that tell what the pets look like. Use some of these words and your own words to describe a pet you like.

TEXT TO WORLD

Research Pets Work with classmates. Use books and other sources to find out how to take care of a pet. Write steps.

Grammar

Possessive Pronouns Some **pronouns** show that something belongs to someone. This kind of pronoun can come before a noun or at the end of a sentence.

Read Together

This is **my** dog.   This dog is **mine**.
I am using **your** chalk.   The chalk is **yours**.
That is **his** shadow.   That shadow is **his**.
I am wearing **her** hat.   This hat is **hers**.

Write the correct pronoun
to finish each sentence.
Use another sheet of paper.

1. I have a dog. Little Cleo is _____**?**_.
   mine   mines

2. This is her dish. The dish is _____**?**_.
   his   hers

3. I whistle. Cleo hears _____**?** whistle.
   my   mine

4. She follows me to _____**?** house.
   your   yours

5. Cleo thinks your toys are _____**?**!
   her   hers

Connect Grammar to Writing

When you proofread your writing, be sure
you have used pronouns correctly.

Narrative Writing

☑ **Organization** When you write sentences for a **story summary,** tell the important events in the order they happened.

Abby wrote a summary of **Whistle for Willie.** Later, she moved one sentence.

Revised Draft

Peter kept trying to whistle.

He practiced in a mirror.

He went into his house.

Writing Checklist

☑ **Organization** Did I tell the events in order?

☑ Do I need to add more important details?

☑ Did I use the correct pronouns?

114

Final Copy

Whistle for Willie

Peter kept trying to whistle.
Then he went into his house.
He practiced in a mirror.
When Peter's mom saw him,
he pretended to be his dad.
Then Peter went outside.
He saw Willie, so he hid
under the carton.
Finally, Peter whistled and
Willie ran to him.
Peter was so happy!

LANGUAGE DETECTIVE

Talk About Words
Work with a partner. Choose one of the sentences. Take out the yellow word. Put in a word that means the same or almost the same thing. Tell how the sentences are the same and different.

Words to Know

Read Together

▶ Read each **Context Card**.

▶ Describe a picture, using the blue word.

1 **ready**
We are ready to pick apples.

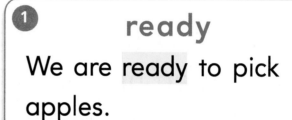

2 **country**
We live in the country.

3 soil

We planted the flowers in the soil.

4 kinds

There are many kinds of butterflies here.

5 earth

She covers the seeds with earth.

6 almost

The apples are almost ripe.

7 covers

Pollen covers the bee.

8 warms

The oven warms our apple pie!

Read and Comprehend

✓ **TARGET SKILL**

Sequence of Events Many selections tell about things in the order in which they happen. This order is called the **sequence of events**. Think about what happens first, next, and last as you read. You can use a flow chart to keep track of the sequence of events.

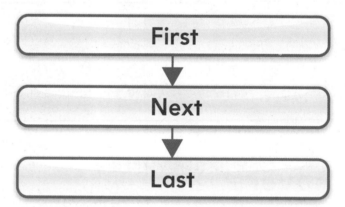

✓ **TARGET STRATEGY**

Question Ask yourself questions as you read. Look for text evidence in the selection to answer your questions.

Life Cycle

A seed is planted. A small plant sprouts up. It grows bigger. Then beans grow on the plant. Inside the beans are more seeds which can be planted! This is the life cycle of a bean plant.

Every living thing has a life cycle. You will read about the life of an apple tree in **A Tree Is a Plant.**

💬 Talk About It

What do you know about how trees change as they grow? Complete the sentences:
I know trees ___. I would like to know more about ___. Talk about your ideas.

- ▸ Listen carefully.
- ▸ Take turns.
- ▸ Ask and answer questions.

119

A Tree Is a PLANT

by Clyde Robert Bulla
Illustrated by Stacey Schuett

☑ GENRE

Informational text gives facts. As you read, look for:
- ▸ information and facts in the words
- ▸ pictures that show details about the real world

Meet the Author
Clyde Robert Bulla

Clyde Robert Bulla lived on a farm and went to a one-room school. He loved to read and write, but he also had to do chores. When he was 10 years old, Clyde entered an essay contest and won a prize! When he grew up, he wrote many books for children.

Meet the Illustrator
Stacey Schuett

As a child, Stacey Schuett loved to ride her horse, Snorky, and be able to observe nature. She puts a lot of what she remembers in her drawings and paintings.

A Tree Is a Plant

by Clyde Robert Bulla

illustrated by Stacey Schuett

ESSENTIAL QUESTION

What happens to a tree as it grows?

CONIFER

MAPLE

PALMS

PERSIMMON

WILLOW

LEMON

A tree is a plant.

A tree is the biggest plant that grows.

Most kinds of trees grow from seeds

the way most small plants do.

There are many kinds of trees.

Here are a few of them.

How many do you know?

This tree grows in the country.
It might grow in your yard, too.
Do you know what kind it is?
This is an apple tree.

This apple tree came from a seed.

The seed was small.

It grew inside an apple.

Have you ever seen an apple seed?

Ask an adult to help you cut
an apple in two.

The seeds are in the center.

They look like this.

Most apple trees come from seeds
that are planted.
Sometimes an apple tree grows
from a seed that falls
to the ground.

The wind blows leaves over the seed.
The wind blows soil over the seed.

All winter the seed lies
under the leaves and the soil.
All winter the seed lies under
the ice and snow and is
pushed into the ground.

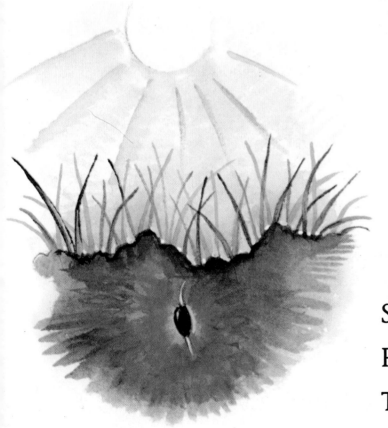

Spring comes.
Rain falls.
The sun comes out
and warms the earth.
The seed begins to grow.

At first the young plant does not
look like a tree.
The tree is very small.
It is only a stem with two leaves.
It has no apples on it.
A tree must grow up before it
has apples on it.
Each year the tree grows.
It grows tall.
In seven years it is so tall that
you can stand under its branches.
In the spring there are
blossoms on the tree.
Spring is apple-blossom time.

ANALYZE THE TEXT

Sequence of Events After many years, what happens to the little plant?

The blossoms last only a few days.

Then they fall to the ground.

Now there are green leaves on the tree.

Among the leaves there are small apples.
The apples are where the blossoms were
before. The apples are green, and they
are almost too small for you to see.
The apples grow slowly.
They grow all during the spring and
the summer.

In the fall they are large and ripe.
They are ready to eat.
We can see the apples and the leaves
on the branches.
We can see the branches growing
out of the trunk.
We can see the trunk
growing out of
the ground.

We can see the bark of the tree.
The bark covers the branches and
the trunk like a coat.
But there is a part of the tree
that we cannot see.

ANALYZE THE TEXT

Figurative Language Why
do you think the author says
the bark is like a coat?

133

We cannot see the roots.

They are under the ground.

Some of the roots are large.

Some of them are as small as hairs.

The roots grow like branches under the ground.

Roots hold the trunk in the ground.
Roots keep the tree from falling when
the wind blows.
Roots keep the rain from washing
the tree out of the ground.

Roots do something more.

They take water from the ground.

They carry the water into the trunk of the tree.

The trunk carries the water to the branches.

The branches carry the water to the leaves.

Hundreds and hundreds of leaves
grow on the branches.
The leaves make food from water and air.
They make food when the sun shines.
The food goes into the branches.
It goes into the trunk and roots.
It goes to every part
of the tree.

Fall comes and winter is near.

The work of the leaves is over.

The leaves turn yellow and brown.

The leaves die and fall to the ground.

Now the tree is bare.

All winter it looks dead.

But the tree is not dead.

Under its coat of bark, the tree is alive.

Spring comes again.   Rain falls.

The sun warms the earth.

The tree blossoms, and new leaves grow.

As long as it lives, the apple tree grows.

As long as it lives, the apple tree blossoms

in the spring, and apples grow on it.

When do you like apple trees best?

In spring when they are covered with blossoms?

In summer when they are covered with leaves?

In winter when they are bare?

Or in fall when they are covered with apples?

Dig Deeper

Read Together

Use Clues to Analyze the Text

Use these pages to learn about Sequence of Events and Figurative Language. Then read **A Tree Is a Plant** again.

Sequence of Events

The order in which events happen is the **sequence of events**. **A Tree Is a Plant** tells about the events in the life of a tree. The apple tree begins as a seed. What happens next? When the tree is big, what happens to it in the spring, summer, fall, and winter? Use a flow chart to show the order of important events.

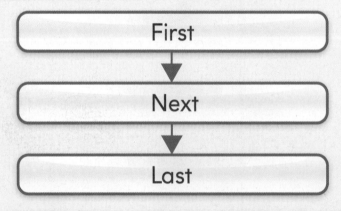

First

↓

Next

↓

Last

Figurative Language

Authors sometimes tell how two things are the same by using the word **like** or **as**. This word choice is called a **simile.**

In **A Tree Is a Plant,** the author says that the roots are **as small as hairs**. Do you think this means the roots are thick or thin? Describe how you picture the roots. What else does the author say the roots are like?

Your Turn

RETURN TO THE ESSENTIAL QUESTION

Turn and Talk

What happens to a tree as it grows? Talk about the order of events in **A Tree Is a Plant.** Could the author have used a different order? Why or why not? Use text evidence from the selection in your answers.

💬 Classroom Conversation

Talk about these questions with your class.

1 Why are a tree's roots important?

2 How do leaves help a tree?

3 What is the order of the seasons? How does the apple tree change during the seasons?

WRITE ABOUT READING ·········

Response Make a chart that shows the steps in an apple tree's life. Draw what the tree looks like at each step. Label the parts of the tree.

   Then write a fact you learned about how apple trees grow. Use text evidence, such as words and pictures in the selection, for ideas.

leaves

branch

bark

trunk

Writing Tip

Add labels to give more information about pictures.

INFORMATIONAL TEXT

Read Together

Grow, **Apples**, Grow!

Grow, Apples, Grow!

Every apple tree starts with a tiny apple seed. An apple tree grows roots, which take in water and food from the soil. The apple tree also grows leaves, which make food from sunlight.

apple

seed

In the spring, apple trees blossom, or grow flowers.

The flowers drop off, and apples grow in their place.

In the fall, the apples are ready to be picked.

People make many kinds
of foods from apples.

Apples may be sweet, or tart,
or soft, or crisp, or crunchy.
But one thing apples always are is
munchy,

munchy,

munchy!

Compare Texts

Read Together

TEXT TO TEXT

Compare Both selections are about apple trees. How are the pictures alike and different? Make a chart. Write text evidence from each selection about apple trees during one season.

Spring	
A Tree Is a Plant	Grow, Apples, Grow!

TEXT TO SELF

Write a Story Pretend that your class hiked to an apple tree and back. Write a story. Tell what happened in order.

TEXT TO WORLD

Look It Up Find out more about trees. Write the most interesting fact you learn. Draw a picture of it.

Grammar

Indefinite Pronouns There are special **pronouns** that stand for the names of people or things. They do not take the place of a noun for a certain person or thing, though.

Read Together

Anyone can pick apples.

I want to learn **everything** about apples.

Someone planted the apple seeds long ago.

Who has **something** to put the apples in?

Everyone at home loves apples!

Try This!

Use a pronoun from the box to complete each sentence. There may be more than one right answer. Write each sentence on a sheet of paper. Take turns reading your sentences with a partner.

anyone	something	someone
everything	everyone	

1. We saw _____ picking an apple.

2. _____ can eat apples.

3. I like _____ about apples.

4. _____ rides to the apple farm.

Connect Grammar to Writing

When you proofread your writing, make sure your indefinite pronouns make sense where they are used.

Narrative Writing

✔️ **Development** When you plan a **story,** think of your characters. How do they look? What do they like? What problem do they have?

Read Together

Deval drew pictures of his characters. Then he wrote clear details about them.

Exploring a Topic

fly fast   friends

like apples

Prewriting Checklist

✔️ Did I write details to describe my characters?

✔️ Did I plan a problem my characters will solve?

✔️ Does my story have a beginning, a middle, and an ending?

Look in Deval's Story Map for details about his characters and the problem they will solve. Now make a Story Map for your own story. Use the Checklist.

Story Map

Characters	Setting
2 bees named Burt and Al	a beehive

Plot

Beginning

bees are best friends

fly fast

like apples

Middle

Al moves (problem!)

bees talk on the phone

Ending

Burt brings apples to Al

Lesson
25

The New Friend
by Maria Pascal · Illustrations by Ed Martinez

Symbols of Our Country

🔍 LANGUAGE DETECTIVE

Talk About Words
Work with a partner.
Read the sentences on
the **Context Cards.**
Turn two of the
sentences into just
one sentence.

Words to Know

Read Together

▶ Read each **Context Card.**

▶ Use a blue word to tell
about something you did.

1   city

They moved to the city
from the country.

2   myself

I took the box into the
house all by myself.

3 school

He met many new friends at school.

4 party

They had a party for their new classmate.

5 seven

She will bring seven apples to school.

6 buy

She will buy a plant for her friend.

7 please

"Please play with us," they said.

8 family

They invited the family to come in.

Read and Comprehend

☑ **TARGET SKILL**

Understanding Characters Remember that you can learn a lot about what story **characters** are like from their words and actions. Use what the characters say and do as clues. Figure out how they feel and why they act the way they do. You can list the clues, or text evidence, on a chart.

Words	Actions	Feelings

☑ **TARGET STRATEGY**

Summarize Stop to tell about the important events as you read.

162

Learning About Our Country

We live in the United States of America. People have come to this country from all over the world. You learn about our country at school. You can read books about our country, too.

You will read about a boy who moves to the United States in **The New Friend.**

💬 **Think | Write | Pair | Share**

What do you know about our country? Think about it. Complete the sentence: Our country is ___. Share with a partner. Act out what you know.

Lesson 25

ANCHOR TEXT

✓ GENRE

Realistic fiction is a story that could happen in real life. As you read, look for:
- ▶ characters who act like real people
- ▶ events that could really happen

Meet the Author

María Puncel

María Puncel lives in Spain. She writes her books in Spanish. Many of them have been translated into English, including **El Amigo Nuevo**.

Meet the Illustrator

Ed Martinez

Ed Martinez grew up with a painter in the family. His father was an artist! As a boy, Mr. Martinez got started by drawing horses. Now he draws pictures for magazines and books.

The New Friend

by María Puncel • illustrations by Ed Martinez

ESSENTIAL QUESTION

What can you learn from someone who is from another country?

Martin, Luis, and I lived in the city. Next door was an old house. No one had lived there for a long time.

ANALYZE THE TEXT

Narrator Who is the narrator? Why do you think so?

One day a work crew came with pails and brushes. They started to wash and paint the empty house.

After they were done, and the paint had dried, the house looked pretty and new.

The next day a big truck pulled up. It was full of crates and boxes. A crew unloaded the boxes off the truck. A new family would soon live there.

Today Luis went over to the house next door.
He met a boy called Makoto. Then we all met
Makoto. Makoto was seven years old—just
like us.

Before long, we found out that Makoto played
soccer. He could keep running and running.
He was good at learning things, too. He learned
all of our names by the end of the game.

Soon Makoto's family was all moved in. We met his mother and father. They were glad that Makoto had made some new friends.

While Makoto's mother and father went to buy food, Makoto stayed and played with us.

When Makoto's mother and father rejoined us, Martin, Makoto, and I helped them carry the bags into the house.

Makoto said he would show us around his house. Then we went up to look at Makoto's room.

Makoto still had a lot of boxes to unpack. He had some nice toys and kites. He said that on the next windy day, we could bring his kites outside and fly them. He said I could fly a kite by myself.

Then we went outside to look
at Makoto's pictures from Japan.
He had them in a green book.

On the first page, we saw Makoto's old house
in Japan. On the next page, we saw Makoto's
family in Japan. The last page had pictures
of Makoto's friends. They showed Makoto's
seventh birthday party. Makoto said he
wishes we could meet his old friends.

At the end of the day, Makoto's mother and father repaid us for helping—with cookies! We said "please" and "thank you" and ate up.

Makoto's father said he had a new job in the city. Makoto would be going to our school. We were all glad about that!

ANALYZE THE TEXT

Understanding Characters
What are Makoto's parents like? Use text evidence and the pictures.

We said good-bye to Makoto and his mother and father. Then we went home to our families. We were glad to have a new friend next door.

Dig Deeper

Use Clues to Analyze the Text

Use these pages to learn about Understanding Characters and the Narrator. Then read **The New Friend** again.

Understanding Characters

You read about a **character** named Makoto in **The New Friend**. Think about what Makoto says and does in the story. You can use these clues, or text evidence, to figure out how he feels and what he is like. List clues about Makoto and the other characters to help you understand them better. Use a chart like this one.

Words	Actions	Feelings

Narrator

Sometimes a character tells the story. This character is the **narrator**. The narrator may use words like **I**, **me**, and **we**.

Which character in **The New Friend** do you think is telling the story? Why do you think so? Look for text evidence in the words and pictures to help you figure it out.

Your Turn

 **What can you learn from someone who is from another country?** What do you think the boys in the story will learn from Makoto? Describe how the boys and Makoto feel about each other. Use text evidence.

 Classroom Conversation

Talk about these questions with your class.

1 How do you think Makoto feels about moving to a new place?

2 What are Makoto's new friends like?

3 How would you make a new friend feel welcome?

WRITE ABOUT READING

Response Read pages 170–171 again. What do you learn about Makoto? Use evidence from the words and pictures in the story for more clues about what Makoto is like. Write sentences to tell your opinion of Makoto. Give reasons.

Writing Tip

Your last sentence should be a nice ending. It can tell your opinion again.

Read Together

Symbols of Our Country

Informational text gives facts about a topic. It can be a newspaper, magazine, or textbook. Read to find facts about symbols of our country.

TEXT FOCUS

Headings are titles for different parts of a selection. They tell what the section is about. What headings do you see in this selection? What information do they give?

Symbols of Our Country

by Agatha Jane

We live in the United States of America. This city is Washington, D.C. It is the capital of the United States. You can see and learn a lot here. Let's go!

American Flag

The flag is a symbol of the United States. The red and white stripes stand for the first thirteen states. The stars stand for each state that is part of the United States now.

Washington Monument

George Washington was our first President. This tall building is named for him. This painting of George Washington is in the White House.

Lincoln Memorial

Abraham Lincoln was our sixteenth President. You can see his statue at the Lincoln Memorial.

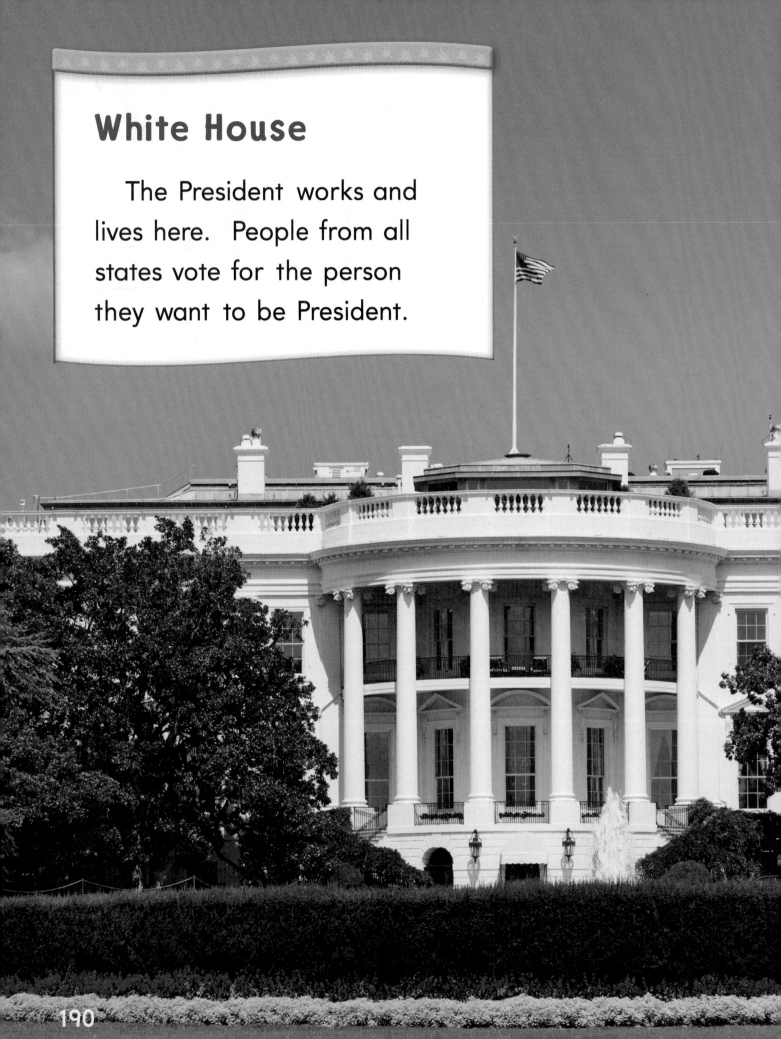

White House

The President works and lives here. People from all states vote for the person they want to be President.

Capitol Building

Voters from each state elect people to represent them. This is where they make laws.

Supreme Court

Judges work here. They decide how laws should be followed.

Constitution

Mount Rushmore

You can see symbols of our country all over the United States. We are very proud of our country!

Liberty Bell

Statue of Liberty

Compare Texts

Read Together

TEXT TO TEXT

Look It Up What country is Makoto's family from? Find out about that country's flag. Find out about other symbols of that country.

TEXT TO SELF

Describe a Symbol What American symbol do you like best? Tell what it looks like. Give reasons why you like it.

TEXT TO WORLD

Connect to Social Studies What changes happen when people move to a new country? What stays the same? Talk with a group.

Grammar

Contractions A **contraction** is a short way of writing two words. This mark (') takes the place of missing letters. It is called an **apostrophe**.

Read Together

It is a very big truck!
It's a very big truck!

He is helping his dad.
He's helping his dad.

This box **is not** too heavy.
This box **isn't** too heavy.

I **do not** know what is in it.
I **don't** know what is in it.

194

Read each sentence. Write the contraction for the underlined words. Use another sheet of paper.

1. <u>I am</u> happy to meet a new friend.

2. Today <u>he is</u> moving next door.

3. Jamal <u>is not</u> finished unpacking.

4. I <u>do not</u> know what games he likes.

5. His toys <u>are not</u> on the shelves yet.

Connect Grammar to Writing

When you proofread your writing, be sure you have written contractions correctly.

Narrative Writing

✓ **Conventions** A good **story** usually has some short sentences and some long ones. Deval drafted a story about two friends. Later, he made a long sentence by joining two short sentences with **and.**

Revised Draft

Burt picked a bunch of
apples, and He packed them up.
    ^

Revising Checklist

✓ Did I write some short and long sentences?

✓ Does my story have a beginning, a middle, and an ending?

✓ Did I write the exact words a character says?

✓ Did I use time-order words?

Find short and long sentences in Deval's story. Use the Checklist to revise your own draft.

Final Copy

Best Friends

Burt and Al lived in a beehive. They were best friends. They both flew fast. They both liked apples. Then Al moved south where there were no apples. Al called Burt. "I'm so sad," he said. Soon they had an idea. Burt picked a bunch of apples, and he packed them up. Then he got on a jet. When Burt got to Al's house, Al was so happy! The friends had juicy apples to celebrate.

Write a Story

TASK Look at **Garden Good Guys** and **Amazing Animals.** Then write a story to share with classmates. Use animals from both texts as your characters.

PLAN ···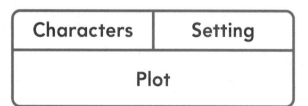

Gather Information Talk with a group about the two texts. Tell facts about the animals. Tell what they might do in a make-believe story.

Use the tools in your eBook to remember facts about the animals.

Write your story ideas on a story map.

- Pick an animal from each text for your characters.

- Describe them. Use facts and your imagination.

- Describe the setting.

- What is the problem? How will it be solved?

Characters	Setting
Plot	

Write your
draft in
*my*WriteSmart.

Write Your Story Use your story map for ideas. Follow these steps.

Beginning

Begin your story. Where are the characters? What is the problem? Write dialogue to tell what the characters say. Use these sentences for ideas.

Once upon a time, there was a _____ and a _____.

One day, _____. "_____!" said _____.

⬇

Middle

Tell what happens next. How do the characters try to solve the problem? Make your story exciting! Use time-order words to tell when events happen. Use pronouns so you don't say characters' names too much.

Next, _____ and _____ _____.

Then, they _____!

⬇

Ending

Tell how the problem is solved. Then write a sentence to end your story. Here are ideas.

• Tell the lesson the characters learned.
• Tell how they feel about each other.

Review Your Draft Read your writing and make it better. Use the Checklist.

my WriteSmart

Ask a partner to read your draft. Talk about how you can make it better.

☑ Did I tell a story about animals from the two texts? Does my story have facts from the texts?

☑ Does my story have a beginning, middle, and ending?

☑ Did I use time-order words?

☑ Did I use pronouns for variety?

☑ Did I use quotation marks (" ") around the words characters say?

Share Make a final copy of your story. Add pictures. Pick a way to share.

- Make your story into a book.
- Read your story to a group.

Duck and Dragonfly's Big Trip

Unit 5   High-Frequency Words

21 The Garden

few	window
loudly	story
noise	shall
night	world

24 A Tree Is a Plant

kinds	earth
country	almost
warms	ready
soil	covers

22 Amazing Animals

learning	young
begins	follow
until	years
eight	baby

25 The New Friend

city	seven
myself	buy
school	please
party	family

23 Whistle for Willie

house	father
along	again
together	nothing
boy	began

Glossary

A

adult

An **adult** is a grown-up. A crossing guard is often an **adult** who helps children cross a busy street.

amazing

Something **amazing** will cause surprise. It is **amazing** to see a shooting star.

B

blossoms

A **blossom** is a small flower on a tree or plant. The pink cherry **blossoms** will fall and then cherries will grow.

brushes

A **brush** is a tool that is used for scrubbing. We use the **brushes** to scrub the floors.

C

camel

A **camel** is a large animal with a long neck and one or two humps. We saw a **camel** at the animal park.

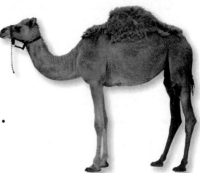

candles

A **candle** is made of wax, and a string in the middle is burned for light. When the electricity went off, we lit **candles** to help us see.

carton

A **carton** is a box used to store things. Martin packed his toys in the **carton** before he moved.

center

The **center** of something is the middle. There is a pit in the **center** of a peach.

color

A **color** is a kind of light that comes from an object to our eyes. Green is my favorite **color**.

crates

A **crate** is a kind of box used for packing things. We packed the books in **crates** to move them.

crew

A **crew** is a group of people who work together.
The **crew** worked together to build the ship.

D

dolphin

A **dolphin** is a sea animal related
to a whale. The **dolphin** swam
next to the ship.

E

empty

Empty means with nothing inside. When I opened the
box, it was **empty**.

errand

An **errand** is a short trip you take to do something.
I ran an **errand** for my mom.

F

frightened

To be **frightened** means to be scared. My dog is **frightened** by thunderstorms.

G

grocery

A **grocery** store is where you buy food. Luke stopped at the **grocery** store to pick up some bread for dinner.

H

happened

To **happen** means to take place. Mr. Chow read about what **happened** in the park.

hundreds

One **hundred** is a number that is one more than ninety-nine. The term **"hundreds"** means very many. There must be hundreds of ants in that big anthill!

O

of course

The words **of course** mean that something is expected to happen. It's lunchtime, and so **of course** we'll have lunch.

P

pails

A **pail** is something you use to carry things. The people used **pails** to carry water to put out the fire.

pocket

A **pocket** is a small bag of cloth. I always keep my money in the **pocket** of my pants.

poems

A **poem** is a kind of writing that often has rhyming words and rhythm. I will write funny **poems** about driving a car to a star and swimming in the sea with a big bee.

polar bear

A **polar bear** is a large white bear that lives where it is cold. A **polar bear** will roll in the snow to clean its fur.

porcupine

A **porcupine** is an animal that is covered with long sharp quills. Most animals will leave a **porcupine** alone.

R

rejoined

To **rejoin** means to get together again. We **rejoined** the group after we finished our chores.

repaid

To **repay** means to give something back. I **repaid** my brother the money he loaned me.

S

seventh
If something is **seventh**, that means that there are six things before it. Saturday is the **seventh** day of the week.

shadow
A **shadow** is a dark area with light around it. The sun made a **shadow** behind the tree.

shouted
When you **shout**, you speak very loudly. When we won the game, everyone **shouted**, "Hooray!"

soccer
Soccer is a game where players kick a ball. Nina was a very good **soccer** player because she was fast.

staked
To **stake** means to use a pointed stick to help something stand up. Andrea **staked** the plant to help it grow straight.

stroked

To **stroke** means to rub gently. Matt **stroked** the puppy to make it calm down.

T

themselves

Themselves means those people or animals. As animals get older, they can take care of **themselves**.

toes

Toes are the parts of the foot that help people and animals walk. People have five **toes** on each foot.

U

unloaded
To **unload** means to take off or take out. The woman **unloaded** the bags of food from the car.

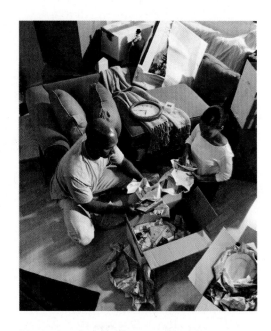

unpack
To **unpack** means to take out of a box or a suitcase. We started to **unpack** the boxes in the kitchen.

W

whirled
To **whirl** means to spin or to turn in circles. My little brother **whirled** and whirled until he was dizzy.

Acknowledgments

Credits